SNOW ANGELS

A TRUE STORY

CHERYL BARINGER

Copyright © 2023 by Cheryl Baringer

All rights reserved. This book or any portion thereof may not be reproduced or used in any manner whatsoever without the express written permission of the publisher except for the use of brief quotations in a book review.

ISBN 978-1-7348968-7-9 (paperback)
ISBN 978-1-7348968-8-6 (ebook)

Formatter/Editor: Pamela Gossiaux
Cover design: Adam Martinelli

Published in the United States by Tri-Cat Publishing.
Chelsea, MI

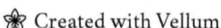 Created with Vellum

SNOW ANGELS

Sleet rattled the old hospital's windows, leaving ghosts of ice behind. Thin frozen shapes caught between fraying screens and yellowing glass attempted a half-hearted escape. The radiator in my mother's room competed with the whir and click of contraptions. From her window I watched a steady stream of visitors race across the top floor of the parking structure, keys out and collars up, buffering oncoming darkness and record-breaking wind chill.

By midnight, blowing snow erased their steps, leaving a shimmering blanket beneath streetlamps. Curling into the peeling vinyl chair, I contemplated the pristine expanse four floors below. *A terrific opportunity for snow angels.* I could probably make it there and back before the screeching wheels of the medicine cart paused by her doorway at 1 a.m. I'd race out and sink my teeth into the biting air and let myself free fall backward, safe in the knowledge there would be no pain. Only the fluffy crunch as the weight of my limbs compressed the snow, and the sheer freedom of swirling my arms wide to create the wings. This woman lying behind me, motionless, had taught me the magic when I was only four.

"Stand by me and hold my hand," she'd joyfully instructed. "That's it, now just trust me and fall!"

I could still remember my delight when she'd pulled me up, and I turned to see the impressions left behind. Two connected angels, one so much smaller.

"There! You see? They're our Guardian Angels! They're always around, but you can only see them when it snows," she'd giggled into that still winter morning, brushing the snow from my hair and snowsuit. "Even after the snow melts, they'll still be watching over us."

If I could only make it down there, maybe I could make my angel appear. From my place flat in the snow, I'd cast a wish up on my frosty breath, and summon him. Then I would search for the constellations my Father had traced across hundreds of violet nights. I was reaching for my coat and gloves when she coughed. Deep racking sounds filled the room, and I remembered. There were no angels, no use in wishing. I winced, hoping she couldn't feel her pain, or mine, in her coma.

Only two evenings before, her petite, graceful hand had reached out for mine. Our roles had slowly changed over the past several years. I was now her sole protector, inheriting that responsibility from my father when he'd died three months before. An agonizing battle with a lingering disease had finally ended for him, leaving my mother heartsick and adrift.

Weaving between cords and tubing, I slid onto the narrow bed beside her, and lay my head softly against her shoulder. She was cocooned in the coarse brown hospital blanket, hands resting across her chest. I moved them quickly so as not to envision anything more permanent. With every fiber of my soul I willed her fingers to rise and stroke my hair as they had so many times before. Instead, my hand caressed thin blue veins these vultures were continuously poking. Occasionally my denial would wane from sheer exhaustion, and the truth rose up, bitter in my throat. My mother was leaving me. Both parents would be gone in the span of a season. The future stretched ahead empty and shattered without her.

I wish I could say I responded with acceptance and dignity. I didn't. While my ever-dignified, faithful mother would have graciously bid farewell to a life well lived, I met the sudden shock with the rampant barking of a drill sergeant. *She's too cold! Are you incompetent?! Don't stick her with that needle again! If you hurt her, I will have your job!* And so the week progressed. From the relief at hearing the initial report of a mild stroke accompanied by her brave smile to my terror as I read the increasingly somber expressions of our family's internist and her neurologist. One minute she was laughing, and then in the blink of an eye, she slid into a coma. You can split an atom but dare to resolve blood clots in the brain stem and you will find such cutting edge remedies as aspirin.

On the third night her ragged breathing drove me to the smokers' alcove outside the first floor. There I found kindred spirits and an old habit I thought I'd kicked. We flocked together for quick moments of escape, entwining our fraying threads of hope. I was bitterly giving the three-drag synopsis of my mother's shocking stroke to a random gathering when a man spoke from the shadow of the doorway.

"Why don't you try the chapel? Just inside and to the right." He exhaled a cloud and let his stub arc into the darkness. "Open 'round the clock."

"I don't think you heard me," I said, clearing my throat loudly at the inconvenience of having to explain the obvious. "My mother is *dying*. It's too late for a miracle."

"Oh, I'm not worried about your mom. She'll be fine. It's you who seems to need the help. You're the one." He tossed his gaping hood up and over hair graying at the temples.

"Well, thanks, Christmas Future, for the free advice." I lit a second Marlboro and inhaled deeply. "But spare me the sanctimonious lecture. With three hours of sleep in as many days, I can't really work introspection into my agenda. Now, if you'll excuse me..." I reconsidered the freshly lit cigarette and ground it into the black slush at my feet.

"Worth a try! You don't have to shoulder this alone." he said. I rolled my eyes right at him and bolted as soon as the electric doors slid open, then rushed to the elevator before the tears burned the back of my eyes. I'd made a rule. Crying was only allowed in elevators. You couldn't be too careful with tears in circumstances like these. Once begun, they may never end. *My God, are people nuts? Shoving their cheery religious panacea down your throat when what you really need is a stiff drink and a place to hide.*

The night passed in sirens, intercom pages and jarred wakings from fragmented dreams. The blue of approaching dawn began to shape the room. Doctors would be making their early rounds soon, crisp and rushed in charcoal pinstripes, white jackets and expensive aftershave. They seemed to glance at their Rolexes often, making sure they were winning the daily race. I felt like a beggar. *Please, sir, may I have a crumb of your time? Just a crumb of time for a dying woman?* My own serious suits and studious black frames had been replaced by the powerless uniform of grief, layers of wrinkled clothing accessorized with shadowed eyes and unwashed hair. I'd spent three nights on the floor by her bed, reaching up through metal slats, holding her hand. She could no longer speak, but I hoped she could still feel my warmth. I begged her not to leave with a grip that was probably too tight, and talked about the fun we'd have when she awoke.

Mid-morning and the parking lot began to fill again. Good thing I hadn't invested any time in those frozen angels. They would have been violated by a convoy of tires spewing black sludge. It was beginning to sleet again. An ice storm was predicted with more snow as an encore.

"Good morning, Mary!" It's time to rise and shine for your therapy!"

I whirled around in disbelief and stood glaring at the invading gaiety, a petite young woman with clipboard and stethoscope. She was shaking my mother's toes in an effort to rouse her. I sprang into action, hauling her from the room.

"Don't touch my mother!" I growled. "Can't you see she's...sleeping."

"Well, I'm sorry, Miss, but I really must adhere to her therapy schedule. It's excellent for circulation and extremely beneficial to the recovery prognosis in general..."

"My God, are you the poster child for Ineptitude? You are, aren't you." I exhaled an exaggerated sigh. "Assuming you can read, please note the DNR on her doorway in large, clearly marked letters. It's not the Department of Natural Resources. It means DO NOT RESUSCITATE. My mother is in a coma. I...we've...they've just disconnected life support. I highly doubt she'll find your therapy beneficial."

"Oh? Well...my goodness. But I have her right here." She pointed to seemingly infallible paperwork. "The computer indicated...um, I'll have to verify this, you know. It clearly states here on my roster that Mary..."

Yanking the offending clipboard from her hands, I focused her attention on the daggers in my bloodshot eyes. "She's my mother. My *moth-er*. Do you think I could possibly be mistaken?"

"No, I suppose not. ...well, ok then, I...I hope you have a nice day." With that she began to back away toward the safety of the nurses' station.

"Have a *nice day*?!" I asked loudly, in a tone that would peel paint, and continued, "Yes, I'll do that, and maybe there are some folks in the morgue downstairs who might benefit from your therapy. Oops, nope, too late for them too." I slammed her clipboard down on a cart and retreated back to my mother, unfolding the pages of her Living Will for the hundredth time. It clearly prevented what were considered heroic measures, but it failed to mention the hopelessness and despair the *Executor* would feel. My name and signature were above that title on the last page, but through tears I saw 'Executioner'.

I'd first seen this document years earlier when my parents had presented it to me at their kitchen table over beers. My dad had joked, "You're all we have, you know. Our one and only. Don't you dare let us down when the time comes, or I promise, I'll come back and haunt you." This was no longer some hypothetical situation I'd relegated to the back of my mind. This was real, and the time had come. Hot tears of disbelief began to flow again, and my blood began to itch for another cigarette. After an entire year of not smoking, it had taken only two to resurrect the old monster of addiction. And I didn't give a damn. I wanted to throw a punch at God. I could think of no one else to blame. "I'll be back in just a minute, Mom." *Academy Award Nominee for Best Cheerful Tone in a Dire Circumstance.*

Leaning against the elevator's glaring brass interior, I begged the numbers to reach one without stopping. I was in luck and sprinted for fresh air, but the sliding hospital doors opened to a horizontal wall of stinging sleet. Scurrying people parted around me, shooting curious glances in my direction. No energy to face the weather, I wandered away and found myself in the last pew of the tiny warm chapel. I'd been here three days before. Praying, raging, bargaining, accusing. Pounding my fists on the polished wood, I'd hurled my despair into the empty sanctuary. The man I'd encountered while smoking was wrong. No help was available here, only the unblinking plaster stares of patron saints guarding candles in red glass. Where in the hell were those guardian angels my mother was always talking to now? "Where *are* you?" I pleaded one last time. Not here, certainly. Shrugging in abject defeat, I left, looking for angels elsewhere.

I wilted back into the cracked vinyl armchair and began a mental list of friends and family who deserved an update. The payphone at the end of the hall saw constant action; I would find it available after visiting hours. My mother's tortured breathing had finally calmed to what appeared a peaceful slumber, and I rose to gently comb the tangles from her silky silver hair. It was matting now, but still held the style of her last weekly appointment. Her high cheekbones were prominent, and I softly touched the contours of her face, ordering my fingertips to remember their delicate shape. "I've scheduled your hair appointment for next week. And told the gals you might not be at bowling. Called your zany neighbor –says he'll fill your bird feeder 'til you get home. And you can believe I'm keeping your doctors in line."

Tears dripped off the end of my nose onto her pillow as I tried to steady my voice. "Say listen, Mom, if you really have to go, I'll understand. I won't be mad, I promise. Even if you miss Dad so much that you *want* to leave, I'll understand. I guess I just keep hoping this is a dream. But I can't wake up." I bit my lower lip hard before continuing. "And I can't wake *you* up. Oh, Mom, I have so many questions. What if I get pregnant? Who will be the Grandma? I don't know the Christmas Slush recipe…and we have reservations for a spa day in March. It was going to be a surprise…and you're the only one who remembers my childhood. It will be lost and gone forever. If you have to go, oh God, I'll feel that at least ten years have been stolen from us. No, twenty." They blurred to irrelevance. "Are you sure you have to go? I guess I thought one of your angels would come, maybe bring us a miracle...."

Another worker on a mission appeared in the doorway soundlessly, an elderly man in a crisp white jacket and pants. *What now? I don't have the strength to deliver another tongue lashing. Especially not to this kind-eyed senior citizen.*

"Hello, there. I only need to come in for a moment." His eyes were warm and confident, his voice familiar. When had I heard him speak recently?

"Look...she's been poked and prodded enough. I know you have a job to do", I sighed, "and I'm sorry I've been mean as a wounded rattler, but it really is pointless. She's...leaving soon and..."

"Shhh...shhh, child. I know. It's just routine..."

I fumed, lowering my voice to a growl . "There is nothing *routine* about this. Bottom line? Nothing you do will change anything. So guess again if you think you're coming near her." Wielding the comb as a weapon, I moved to block this latest intruder from my precious charge. It then occurred to me he sounded like the man I'd encountered smoking, the one who'd recommended the chapel. Before I could ask, he turned toward me and lifted his finger to my lips.

"Shhh, now...don't be so angry. She's coming home and is at peace. This isn't something you can control, much as you'd like. What a beautiful life she's had...so many wonderful memories." He smiled down at her and took her hand in his. "She's a very pretty lady. You have her eyes. Light green like spring leaves." For a moment he seemed lost in thought before continuing. "Now leave me to my task. And please don't stab me with that comb." he teased. "You need a break. Wait in the hallway, and I give you my word, I won't harm her in any way." He delivered this directive in a soothing whisper and gently stroked her hair, mumbling words I could not hear.

Something in his knowing demeanor caused me to give in. I lowered the comb obediently and stepped outside. Quite a new response for me, and one that left me puzzled as I vacantly observed the bustling corridor.

When he emerged, he linked his arm in mine and led me down the hall. "She's resting comfortably now. Can't you see? She's in no pain, I assure you. If you look closely, you'll see her faint smile now and then. Stop fighting this. It's our job to help her on her way."

"Listen, um...Ferdinand?" I looked down at his identification badge and paused, staring at the unusual name. "Yeah, um, I appreciate the kind words, but you really don't have a clue. I know you see this every day, but I've had to make a terrible decision... you don't understand..." I managed, before the words got stuck in my throat.

"Oh, I think I do. It's a tougher road for you than your mom. And most importantly, it's not *your* decision." he said, placing one hand firmly on my shoulder.

"Oh, I get it, you saw her Living Will on the table. Sure, that's what she signed ten years ago, but this is...this is real." I said, still fumbling for some adequate explanation.

"Yes, it's real. And thank God you're here to speak for her as she intended, since she can't. You haven't failed her. You're doing just fine. Besides, you don't strike me as the kinda gal who second guesses important decisions, so buck up now."

"Hmmph. Buck up. How funny. That sounds just like something my dad would've said."

"Must've been a smart guy." With that he winked and went strolling down the hall.

"Hey, wait up a minute." I trotted after him. "What's that you're humming? It sounds familiar."

"Oh, just an old favorite of mine--it's called 'You Belong To Me'."

He turned the corner and was gone. *Strangers stopping by with trite advice. Just breezing in with gritty little pearls of wisdom.* I resented every intrusion but had to admit he'd made me feel better in several minutes than the parade of solemn social workers I continually dismissed. They were already speaking in their quiet funeral parlor voices as they tried to help me understand my anger. As I explained to the last one who'd stopped in—they could all just kiss my anger.

The next two days ticked by in a string of phone calls and whispering visitors I pretended to tolerate as we sat in the grating silence left behind by the absence of the fluids pump and other equipment. I ground my teeth against their sharp gasps at the shocking news. "But she was so *healthy?*" and "Can't they do *something?*" seemed to be the going reaction, and one that left me chilled and guilty. *Why couldn't you save her*, they seemed to be accusing. She'd been the best mother, the best friend, the best person I knew. She'd sprinkled her fairy dust laughter over every fear and heartache I'd known and made certain I found magical reasons to celebrate every day. She was the sparkle in Christmas and the fresh, safe scent of home. Mary knew the tune of every Cardinal in her yard, and my dad always said flowers grew taller toward her encouraging eyes, hoping to please her. Such a gift she'd been to me, to everyone, year after year. And here I was, helplessly unable to return anything in this moment when she needed me most.

"How long before...how much longer?" The words hung in the air between her doctor and me the following morning.

"Probably a day or two. Several at the outside. I really can't say." His pager buzzed impatiently on his hip.

I stared at the polished white floor tiles of the hallway. "She's getting so warm. She's burning up." My face crumpled.

"Yes, that's expected. The absence of fluid therapy. But she's comfortably unaware. It won't be much longer." The pager was checked. "I'll be back tomorrow. We'll know more then." He gave my arm a quick pat and turned to go.

"Wait. Why don't I take her home? She always hated this place. She's been here fifty times with my dad. I want her in her own bed."

"I don't recommend that. You aren't equipped to handle that, and there's no reason to arrange hospice. She really is unaware. She has a private room; it's in her best interest to remain here." He recorded notes onto her chart in a cliché physician's scrawl and softened his clipped tone a notch. "I know this is rather difficult."

"Yes, *rather*."

"Try to get some rest. We don't need to admit you as well." Another impersonal pat.

I nodded wordlessly and returned to her side to count minutes. I must have dozed unknowingly, stretching possessively across her legs. When I awoke, Ferdinand was sitting by her as well, watching us both.

"Gosh, you must have a strange schedule." I yawned. "Seems like you're always hovering around." As promised, he'd checked on us frequently.

"Yep, as luck would have it, I'm working a lot of doubles this week." He tucked in her blankets and caressed her hand.

"It's unbelievably kind of you to spend all of your breaks with us." I unfolded stiffly and rummaged through my purse for change.

"There's no place I'd rather be. Here. Need some quarters for the phone?" He magically produced a handful.

"Oh, no thanks...I can get change in the cafeteria...."

"Why? This should be enough."

"Well...O.K., thanks. Seems like you have exactly what I need almost before I think of it. Say, listen...could you stay with her for just a few minutes longer? So I can call my husband?"

"It'll be my pleasure. When's Randy coming?"

"Tomorrow. Did I mention his name?"

"You must have."

"Wow, I'm so tired I can't even remember what we've talked about." I shook my head to clear the fatigue and continued. "With living in Michigan and being self-employed, I wanted to wait for the right time to have him come. It's tough for us to both be gone." I jingled the coins in my hand. "But he should be here now. He loves her too. My parents never had a son until I married Randy."

Ferdinand smiled and nodded. "Well, get that boy down here. Things will be easier when he comes," he reassured, waving me away to the phone.

When I returned, he patted her cheek good-bye and left humming that old song again. I watched him walk away with a sort of jauntiness to his step. Had anyone else seemed happy at that moment, I would have screamed. But he was genuinely caring and always comforting.

Late the next night, with my husband by my side, my mother gave a final sigh. Her eyelashes fluttered, and I knew she'd gone. I rocked her for a long time, clinging to the weight of her in my arms, pressing her to me. Instead of the waves of anger and sorrow I assumed would flood me, I felt only the privilege of being her daughter.

The next two weeks passed in the blur of wake and funeral, legal paperwork and sympathy cards. Neighborly baked goods in tin foil lined her kitchen counter. I spent hours reading old letters she'd treasured, some from her parents and friends, many from my father while he'd been in Australia and the Philippines during WWII. In one yellowed letter dated December 1944, I found the strangest thing, a request of my father's. He'd written, "Please don't be sad,

Mary. I'll just be gone a little while, and then I'll be coming back for you. I promise. Til then, if you get up to the tavern, have Al play our song. Play 'You Belong To Me'. It took a while, but I found the song on a dusty record album and dropped it onto their old turn table. I played it over and over and was so tired I imagined I heard them singing along. I fed her cardinals and sobbed on her porch. A return to my own home and life in Michigan was fast approaching, but first I needed to pay a visit of gratitude to the man who'd shown such profound compassion to two strangers.

How I hated to walk through those sliding hospital doors to the assault of the scent of floor polish and gift shop flowers, then past the chapel and down the paneled hallway to Hospital Administration. The Human Resources Manager nodded patiently as she input information into her computer.

"No," I sighed. "I'm sorry, I didn't get a last name. And I can't specify his schedule; he was here the entire week. At all different times of day." I pressed on, shifting impatiently, the card and small gift-wrapped box in my lap. "Oh, wait, he did say he was working a lot of doubles that week if that helps."

"Hmmm, that's...unusual. We haven't offered overtime in more than a year. And you don't know his department?"

"No."

"His job title?"

"Nope." I was beginning to feel foolish. "But I really need to thank him. I didn't get to say good-bye."

"Aha. Well, what care did he give your mother?"

"You know, I never really saw him actually do anything. He just...well, he sort of visited us. Three or four times a day." I looked up at the ceiling, hoping to remember more. "Her room was drafty. He covered her with blankets, combed her hair. Brought coffee, quarters..."

She continued tapping on her keyboard, frowning. "Well,

I've cross referenced every field, and I assure you...there has not been anyone by the name of 'Ferdinand' employed by this hospital in the past thirty-six months, including volunteers. I've checked every possible way I can." Efficient eyebrows raised over the top of wire frames. "It was a difficult time for you, I'm sure. Perhaps it was another unusual name beginning with the letter F?"

"No." I shook my head insistently. "No, I saw his nametag. It was Ferdinand. There's no way I would forget that." I laughed. "You see, that was my father's name as well. It was definitely Ferdinand..." I faltered, beginning to feel an impossible thought nudge my skeptical mind. Fading bits of conversation flooded back and I thought out loud. "He said she'd had a wonderful life. Said it wasn't my decision. He knew Randy's name...he hummed their song. So many good memories. He said I had her eyes. Like the color of spring leaves. *But her eyes were closed!* The way he touched her hand, her hair...it was as if...he'd always known her...."

Her fingers hovered above the keyboard, and our eyes locked for a moment as I slowly rose to go.

She sat back in her chair and smiled. "It's not the first time." she said, shrugging her shoulders and tilting her chin as if she knew a secret.

"What do you mean?" I whispered.

"It's not the first time someone's come looking for someone to thank. Someone incredible...who can't be found." she said.

She stood then, opening a drawer and removed cards and letters she'd been unable to deliver and had saved over time. "I've held this position for twenty-two years. At first I tried to explain it away. Some mix up in a grieving loved one's memory, employee payroll errors, something ...anything." She shook her head slowly from side to side, lifting the rubber band and adding my thank-you note to the large stack she held. "I've come to believe there is only one explanation. So you, my dear, are one of the lucky ones. It must be very comforting." There we stood, two women smiling at one another, sharing an unspoken belief in angels.

Now every winter, after the first deep snowfall, I stand and fall weightlessly into the blanket of frozen powder. Free of sorrow, I spread my arms and legs wide, making beautiful wings. I send my laughter, which sounds like hers, along with a prayer of gratitude up on my frosty breath to the winter stars. I am indeed one of the lucky ones. I had them once. I have them still, in ways I could never have imagined. Carefully rising, I move over two feet and fall again. And here they remain, just as she promised, long after the snow has melted. Two perfect angels, wings embracing—watching over my life.

A NOTE FROM THE PUBLISHER

Cheryl is one of my dearest friends, a fellow writer, and one of my strongest prayer warriors. She and I have prayed each other through a lot, and still do. I can't imagine life without her, but I almost found out what that would be like.

On November 1, 2020, in the midst of COVID, Cheryl was rushed to the hospital and underwent emergency surgery for a life-threatening infection. A few weeks earlier, she had gone in for a routine dentist appointment to get her back molar filled. This resulted in a tooth infection that spread. Cheryl's life was spared, but she was left blind, bedridden, and with massive brain damage from a stroke. The doctors though she would die, but Cheryl's always been a tough and determined gal. After a six-month battle in the hospital, over two years of ongoing physical and occupational therapy, and the amazing support and care of her tireless husband Randy, she is getting stronger, and having more coherent conversations. Her mind as well as her body are slowly returning. While she can't often remember names, or what day it is, she remembers this story, and has asked me to publish it.

Despite her circumstances, she is upbeat, a great comfort to me, and continues to tell me and those around her to walk in faith. She loves Jesus and still believes that her guardian angels are watching over her.

I thank God for every day that she is with us.

Pamela Gossiaux
October 2023

ABOUT THE AUTHOR

Cheryl Baringer has always loved to write, and has a large body of work including non-fiction, technical documents, mortgage manuals, press releases, ad copy, website copy and more. She worked as the Director of Communications for an Inc. 500 company for many years, and has been a freelance writer, a jewelry designer, and a veterinary technician. She lives in Michigan on a small lake with her husband and their chocolate lab Cubby. She loves the Lord and knows that her guardian angels are watching over her every day.

www.ingramcontent.com/pod-product-compliance
Lightning Source LLC
Chambersburg PA
CBHW050318100526
44585CB00016BA/1740